Water and Light

Looking through Lenses

by Michinori Murata
photographs by Isamu Sekido

 Lerner Publications Company • Minneapolis

Series Editor: Susan Breckner Rose

This edition first published 1993 by Lerner Publications
Company.
Originally published 1984 in Japanese under the title
Renzu Asobi by Kaisei-Sha Publishing Co., Ltd.

English translation rights arranged with Kaisei-Sha
Publishing Co., Ltd. through Japan Foreign-Rights Centre.

Library of Congress Cataloging-in-Publication Data

Murata, Michinori, 1924-
    [Renzu asobi. English]
    Water and light : looking through lenses / by Michinori
Murata ; photos by Isamu Sekido.
        p.   cm.
    Summary: Explains how such things as a goldfish bowl,
a drop of water, or a magnifying glass act as lenses and
describes the appearance of objects viewed through them.
    ISBN 0-8225-2904-1
    1. Light–Juvenile literature. 2. Light–Experiments–
Juvenile literature. 3. Lenses–Juvenile literature.
4. Water–Optical properties–Juvenile literature. [1. Light.
2. Lenses.] I. Sekido, Isamu, 1946-   ill. II. Title.
QC360.M86   1992
535'.324–dc20   92-19969
                                                        CIP
                                                         AC

Manufactured in the United States of America

1 2 3 4 5 6 98 97 96 95 94 93

What a big goldfish!

It isn't really this big. When light shines through the round bowl of water, some interesting things happen that make the goldfish look bigger than it really is.

We need light in order to see. When light hits a surface, it either bounces off the surface or passes through it. When light hits a surface such as a mirror or a piece of paper, the light bounces back. This bouncing back is called **reflection.**

Light can pass through clear glass or water. When light passes through an object, the light bends. This bending is called **refraction.**

Light bends when it passes from the air into the glass bowl. It bends again when it passes from the glass into the water. The fish you see inside looks bigger because of the bent, or refracted, light.

Our round goldfish bowl full of water is an example of a convex lens. A **lens** is a curved surface that light can pass through. Lenses refract light.

A curved lens that is thicker in the middle than at the edges is called a **convex lens.** A convex lens makes objects look bigger than they really are, like the goldfish bowl makes the goldfish look bigger.

When you look at a pattern through an empty glass, the pattern looks a little wavy and a little bigger. An empty glass is thicker in the middle than at the edges. It is a convex lens.

Do you think the pattern looks different through a glass that is full of water? Try it and see!

Stand this book upright on a table, and place a clear glass of water close in front of this page. You will see that the straight lines of the pattern are now curved. Slowly move the glass backward and forward, from side to side, and up and down. The pattern seems to grow, shrink, and wiggle around.

When light passes from the air into glass, the light is bent, or refracted. And when it passes from the glass into the water, it is refracted again. The glass full of water is a stronger convex lens than the empty glass. The full glass makes the pattern look bigger and more wavy.

A glass of water in the sunlight can make a rainbow. As sunlight passes through a lens, it is refracted. You see a rainbow of colors. Do you know why?

Sunlight is made up of many different colors. When sunlight passes through a lens, each color in it bends at a different angle. The band of colors you see – red, orange, yellow, green, blue, and violet – is called a **spectrum.**

Put a glass of water or a magnifying glass in the sunlight. Like a glass of water, a **magnifying glass** is a convex lens. Move each glass until you find an angle that makes the spectrum spread out. If you tilt the magnifying glass a little, does one color come out more than the others?

A beautiful rainbow stretches across the sky. A **rainbow** is formed when the sun shines on raindrops. Each raindrop is a lens. Each lens refracts sunlight into a tiny spectrum.

10

You can see a rainbow when the sun is shining from low in the sky behind you onto raindrops in front of you.

On a spring or summer morning, you can go outside and find droplets of water on leaves and grasses. Like a glass full of water or a raindrop, a round droplet of water is a convex lens.

Look closely at the water droplets on these clover leaves.
Do the droplets change the way a leaf looks?

Rub a flat glass dish or a sheet of clear plastic with the bottom of a candle. Smooth out the candle wax so you can see through it by rubbing the wax with your thumb.

Drip some water onto the waxed part of the glass dish or plastic sheet. The wax helps the water to stay in droplets instead of running together. The droplets are small convex lenses.

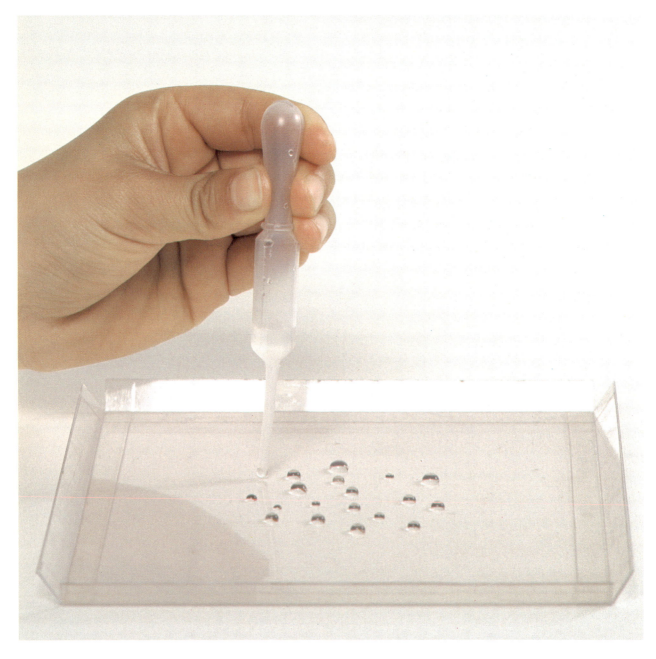

Slide your sheet of small lenses over a picture. Then slide the sheet away. Do the lenses make parts of the picture look larger or smaller? Do they make the picture look different?

Look at leaves and flowers through a larger convex lens–
a magnifying glass. A magnifying glass has a smaller
magnifying power than a water droplet or a round glass
of water. This is because the water droplet and the glass
of water are more curved than the magnifying glass. The
more a lens is curved, the more the light is bent. And the
more the light is bent, the greater the magnifying power
of the lens is.

A greater magnifying power makes an object look bigger, but it also makes an object look more **distorted.** An object is distorted when it seems twisted out of its usual shape.

Look through your magnifying glass into a mirror. What do you see?

Look at some everyday objects you see at home, at school, or outdoors through a magnifying glass. They look bigger than usual, but they don't look as distorted as the goldfish did in its round bowl.

HORSETAIL STEM

BEAN SPROUTS

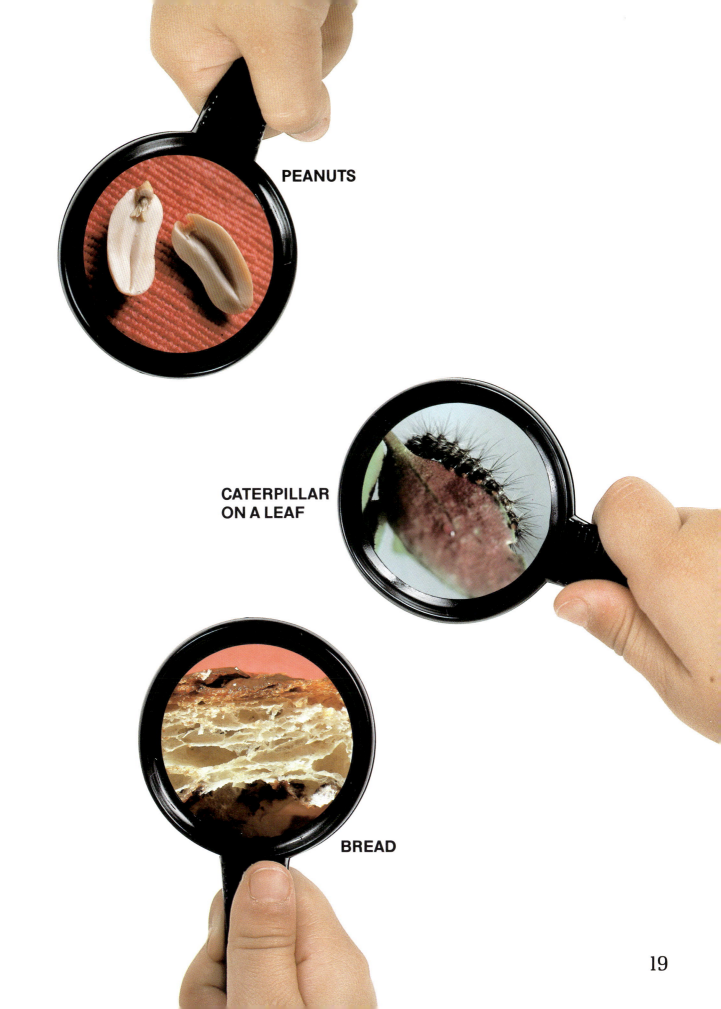

PEANUTS

**CATERPILLAR
ON A LEAF**

BREAD

19

What happens when you tape two magnifying glasses together? Each has the same amount of curve. But as light passes through both magnifying glasses, it is refracted twice. Two magnifying glasses have a greater magnifying power than one. The objects look twice as big as they did on the page before.

HORSETAIL STEM

MOSQUITO UNDER A LEAF

SALT CRYSTALS

Using a magnifying glass, look at all sorts of things around you. Now you can see everyday objects bigger than life. There are surprising discoveries to be made in common things.

BUTTERFLY WING

PIGEON FEATHER

DANDELION WITH A LADYBUG AND AN ANT

Light allows you to see the things around you, from a rainbow in the sky to a mosquito on a leaf. Lenses help you to see these things a little bit differently.

FERN BUD

TISSUE PAPER

FERN LEAF

GLOSSARY

convex lens: a lens that is thicker in the middle than at the edges

distorted: twisted out of its usual shape

lens: a curved, clear surface that light can pass through

magnifying glass: a lens that, when you look through it, makes objects seem bigger

magnifying power: the amount that a lens makes an object seem bigger

rainbow: a band of colors that appears in the sky when sunlight passes through falling rain

reflection: light bouncing back off an object

refraction: light bending as it passes from one clear material into another

spectrum: the band of colors formed when light is broken apart